The P.L.P. Chronicle and Political Poems

The P.L.P. Chronicle
and Political Poems

Norma Ferguson Hill
and Jamie Hill

To order additional copies of this book, contact:
Xlibris Corporation
1-888-795-4274
www.Xlibris.com
Orders@Xlibris.com
102230

CONTENTS

THE "ROOT" OF THE PROGRESSIVE LIBERAL PARTY

Politics is as old as Methuselah. In The Bahamas, the House of the Assembly is where politicians meet to discuss political affairs. Politics is rooted in many Bahamian families. One of the most outstanding, from the 1850s, was Mr. William Campbell Adderley.

Grassroot members from the early 1900s are Mr. Harcourt Malcolm; Hon. Sir George Gamblin; Mr. William P. Adderley, and Mr. L.W. Young in 1912.

The House of the Assembly, during this era, was "rooted" with a powerful speaker named William C.B. Johnson.

The Hon. Thaddeus Toote was elected into the House of the Assembly in 1915. Mr. Harold G. Christie, in 1927, planted his political root. There were countless politicians, springing up with passion, to change The Bahamas, to name a few: Mr. George W. Roberts, in 1934, and Mr. Percy E. Christie in 1935.

When Sir Milo Butler sprang up with power in 1937, it rooted up communities and people to think politically. Mr. Alvin Braynen and Mr. M. Taylor got into "The House."

In 1953, Mr. Charles Rodriguez and Mr. Cyril Stevenson were politically birthed into the Progressive Liberal Party. A few months later, their political sisters (triplets) went into "labor." They were Mrs. Georgianne Symonette, Mrs. Eugenia Lockhart and Mrs. Mary Ingraham.

In 1955 Sir Randol F. Fawkes was pushed to "labor" which introduced him into the P.L.P. Movement.

The Rt. Hon. Sir Lynden Pindling became the Parliamentary leader of The Progressive Liberal Party the same year he was elected to The House of the Assembly. He was elected to a Premier and then Prime Minister for six powerful elections. He transformed the Bahamian people and The Bahamas. The P.L.P. political root sprung because "The man of the century" was a "political anchor."

In 1956, Mr. Clarence Bain, along with many other political radicals were elected into the political movement. They kept the "labor" active.

Mr. Paul Adderley was a full-blooded politician; he proved it in 1961. Also that year, the Hon. Arthur D. Hanna and Mr. Clifford Darling came in the House of Assembly.

Mr. Arthur Foulkes and many other political comrades were inducted to "labor" in The House of the Assembly.

Dr. Doris Johnson was with The Progressive Liberal Party in 1965. She held many first positions for women. She was First Lady in and out the Senate. Mr. Carlton Frances was the first Vice-Chairman of the P.L.P.

Mr. Clement Maynard was "politically rooted" in 1967.

In 1968 Mr. C.V. Wallace-Whitfield stayed "politically correct" with his political family.

The Rt. Hon. Hubert Alexander Ingraham (present Prime Minister of The Bahamas). Served as National General Council of The Progressive Liberal Party in 1975.

The Hon. Janet Bostwick was very powerful and active in the path of the P.L.P. She was the first female attorney general and the first woman elected to The House of the Assembly.

The Progressive Liberal Party birthed many powerful political leaders. In the fifties and sixties, many were elected to The House of Assembly and their names are recorded with their accomplishments in "The Book."

In the1970s, The Progressive Liberal Party was booming with "new birth," with politicians such as: Mr. Loftus Roker; Mr. George Mackey; Hon. Darrell Rolle; Hon. Cynthia Pratt; Dr. Norman Gaye; Allengton Allen; Mr. Charles Carter; Mr. Bradley Roberts; Frank Watson; Mr. Bernard Nottage; Mr. Nevil Wisdom; Mr. Fred Mitchell; and Mr. Obedian Wilchcombe; Mr. Peter Bethel; Mr. Philip Galanis; Mr. Oville Turnquest; Mr. Marvin Pinder; Mr. Jeffrey Thompson; Mr. Sammie Isaacs and Mr. Ervin Knowles.

The Rt. Honorable L.O. Pindling (Prime Minister) wisdom and power grounded in the 1980s. The P.L.P. got rooted up during the 90s and sprung back up at the turn of the millennium.

In 2002, the P.L.P. won an election under the leadership of Mr. Perry Christie (presently opposition leader) who served one term as Prime Minister. Old and new members, such as L. Miller; K. Gibson; A. Maynard-Gibson; K. Smith; D. Gibson; W. Rolle; J. Carey; C. McDonald; D. Coakley; M. Griffin; Y. Turnquest; H. Treco; J. Ritch; G. Hanna-Martin; A. Sear; V. Owens; The P.L.P. grew and grew with members. P. Russell; J. Ingraham; F. Bootie; M. Sawyer; F. Smith; P. Davis; and M. Halkitis. Some P.L.P. family members are: A. Moss; C. Outten; M. Adderley; V. Peet; P. Forbes; C. Johnson; R. Pinder; A. Gray; C. Strachan; P. Bridgewater; and S. Gibson;

The P.L.P. grew with powerful members such as: L. Miller; K. Gibson; C. Pratt; A. Maynard-Gibson; K. Smith; D. Gibson; W. Rolle; J. Carey; C. McDonald; D. Coakley; M. Griffin; Y. Turnquest, to name a few.

Intromemories

I remember the new era,
As if it was yesterday.
I gradually saw the bright golden sun,
Raised in our people and gave us light.
Then I became ray of the flame,
Cause others to beam.
Our prime minister then, was black and proud.
His family was the first whom we adore.
When they got hurt we felt the pain,
When they got blessed, we shared their joy.
In 1970 my family moved to a new home,
Soldier Road was the most excited path,
Because the Pindlings' dwelling were the talk,
Then protocol told it all.
Policemen motorbikes would make some noise,
Why? The Pindlings' were passing by.
We'd run to the side walk with smiles and pride,
Because waving hands were in our reach.
These memories are beyond yesterdays.
Soldier Road you see, was the happiest street,
At Christmas, the lights came on. which made our community.
A star of the land.
Election time the drums beat loud,
After the votes had been counted,
The trumpet would sound, because on Soldier Rd.,
There was a party all the time.
The memories of the Pindlings will always be cherries,
All through the paths, The Progressive Liberal Party take us.

A Blessed Man

Mr. Pindling was a blessed man
Who traveled the globe
He hosted world leaders
As he delighted in the law of the land
He visioned day and night
He had a spiritual foundation
It was focused as he brought
Equal opportunity for all
We all prosper, achieved, and accomplished
Henceforth we have life.

A Political Shepherd

Mr. Pindling was our premier
Whom we did want
He gave us freedom
He led us where we belonged
He rescued us from the U.B.P.
And birth us to P.L.P.
He had no fear,
Because he knew independence was near.
He bestowed the Knights commander
St. Michael and St. George
By her majesty Queen Elizabeth
Such goodness and mercy
Follow him to the end.

Joyful Noise

Cow bells ringing, drums beating, and horns tooting
Was the noise of the land.
Junkanoo
Rushing
As the crowd sings out loud
P.L.P. "All the Way
Mr. Pindling!
He loved us as his people
We were blessed and thankful
He was charming, kind, and a good man.
May his legacy last forever.

A Bahamian Prayer

Father of our nation
Look down from heaven
All the Way!
Can the Bahamians come?
You gave us our 'rights' on this earth
You gave us power!
You fought for our identity
As you gave us dignity
Thank you for your legacy
As we deliver it in unity.

Lord, Send Your Love

Lord, Send Your love
Down on me
Let me feel
Your anointing

Guide my life
Everyday
Lord I ask you
To make a way

It gives me strength
And removes my fears
Your perfect love
Wipes away my tears

Your love, Jesus
Is so wonderful
Let me experience
Joy unspeakable!

Election Commands

Thou shall pray before thy 'party.'
Thou shall vote for the party of one choice.
Thou shall not take voting for granted.
Remember Election Day to go out and vote.
Honor your leaders, because they are the politicians.
Thou shall be honest.
Thou shall not fight.
Thou shall love each other as thou love thyself.

Wisdom

Sir Lynden pursuit in the things his parents taught him.
Knowing what was expected of him, he stayed focused.
At an early age, the word of God was introduced to him.
He was molded into the Bahamas finest patriot.
Through faith which was in Christ.

Campaign Readiness

Ready to walk
Ready to pray
Ready to work
Ready to speak
Ready to distribute
Ready for justice
Ready for equality of opportunity

Mr. Pindling Political Armour

Black and proud
Spiritual and powerful
Emotionally controllable
Phenomenal with people
Smart and charming
Great speaking voice
Courageous in dignity
Excellent leadership.

Things That Minister Pindling Hated

None equal opportunity
Racial barriers
An unhealthy society
Poverty
Progenies in politics
None economic conditions
None educated Bahamians.

Seven P.L.P. Poineers

Sir Milo Butler Sr.
Mr. Clarence Bain.
Mr. Sammie Isaacs.
Mr. Randal Fawkes.
Mr. Cyril Stevenson.
Mr. M. Taylor.
Mr. Arthur Foulkes.

A Politician Fruit

Love
Purpose
Peace
Comrades
Vision
Hope
Power
Faith
Destiny

Taste of Bahamas

Cracked conch and curry
Peas and rice
Macaroni, chicken souse
Oh . . . tastes so nice!

Goombay, Junkanoo punch
Ginger beer, Fruit champagne
And fried plantain to munch

Pineapple tart and Johnnycake
Oh so sweet
Bahamian food is so delicious
I can't wait to eat!

The Ping-A-Tude

Blessed was the man who was blessed by the Lord.
Blessed was his vision, which made him a visionary.
Blessed was his power that influences many people.
Blessed was his attitude, that it helped sealed the spirit of promise.
Blessed was his awareness, it was global.
Blessed was his self-esteem, it impacted the culture.
Blessed was his purpose; it was fulfilled.
Blessed was his love; it was genuine.
Blessed was his leadership as it continues to go "ALL THE WAY."

Some Academics Appearance of Mr. Lynden Pindling

East Street . . . . foundational roots.
Western Senior School . . . . middle school education.
1944 Mrs. McDonald . . . . evening school.
Seventh Day Adventist Church . . . . Pathfinder & Sabbath schools.
The Government High School from 1943-1946 . . . . secondary education.
University of London . . . . law training.
Howard University, Washington D.C. 1973 . . . honorary LL.D doctors of law.
University of Miami 1977 . . . . honorary D.H.L., Doctor of Humane Letters.
Bethune Cookman College 1979 . . . . honorary LL.D., doctor of laws,
by Fisk University, Nashville Tennessee.

❦

How Mr. Pindling Got in the House of Assembly

In 1953, he joined the Progressive Liberal Party.
In 1956, he became a member of parliament.
In 1962, he was elected senior member of the South Central District.
In 1963, became chairman of the P.L.P.
In 1967, he transformed politics victoriously "ALL THE WAY."

❦

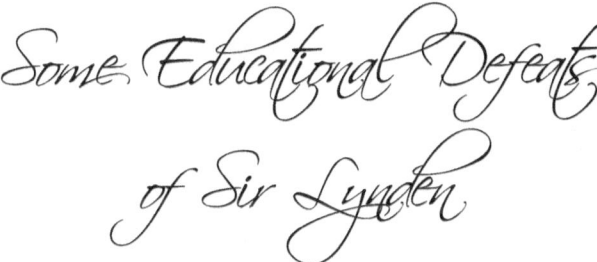

Some Educational Defeats of Sir Lynden

In 1973, The Bahamas Hotel Training College was improved.
In 1974, The College of The Bahamas was established.
In 1980, The Bahamas Technical and Vocational Institute were established.
In 1984, C.O.B. internationally accredited, with U.S. and Canada.
In 1993, the Bahamas General Certificate of Sec. Ed. held its 1st setting.

Sir Lyndens' Twelve Precious Diamonds

Mr. Arnold Pindling.
Mrs. Viola Pindling.
Mrs. (Lady) Marguerite Pindling.
Mr. Obie (Diane) Pindling.
Mr. Leslie Pindling.
Mrs. Michelle (Robert) Sands.
Mrs. Monique (Dr. Daniel) Johnson.
Master Lynden Pindling.
Master Lauren Sands.
Miss. Holly Sands.
Master Andrew Pindling.
Miss. Danielle Johnson.

What a Wonderful Love

The night you said "I love you"
You took a portion of my heart
I pray it's everlasting love,
Which will never grow apart.

There were times I thought it wouldn't last
I thought that we were through
But I fought to keep your heart
That's just what love will do.

I like when you embrace me
And I like your touch
I like when you kiss me
It's never too much.

I like the way you dress
And I like the way you talk
You have a pretty cool swag
I even watch the way you walk.

I've told you that you're handsome
I like the complexion of your skin
I love when we're together
I feel passion from within.

I don't have to question
If your love for me is real
I trust we'll be committed
And do the real deal.

Twelve Architect of Modern Bahamas

Extensions of The Princes Margaret Hospital and 10 clinics on Family Is.
Tourism and the hotels industries improvement.
The new National Insurance Board.
The Great Royal Bahamas Defense Force.
The Bahamas Agricultural and Industrial Corporation.
The Archives Department improvement.
The Water and Sewerage Corporation.
The Mortgage Corporation.
The national flag carrier, BahamasAir
The Bahamas Development Bank and the Bahamas Bank.
The Central Bank of the Bahamas.
The Government-owned Tel-Vision.

Fifteen P.L.P. Faithful Leaders

Mr. Paul Adderly
Hon. Arthur Hanna
Hon. Livingston Coakley
Mr. Carlton Frances
Sir Clement Maynard
Hon. George A. Smith
Mr. Kendal Nottage
Dame Dr. Doris Johnson
Mr. Jeffrey Thompson
Hon. A. Loftus Roker
Mr. George Macky
Mr. Charles Carter
Mr. Peter Bethel.
Hon. Darrell Rolle
Hon. Dr. Norman Gay.

Mr. Pindling Last Words in Parliament

Monday, July. 1997,
Friends, forty years with honorable members
which seem like yesterday.
It was by His grace and blessings,
that I accomplished much.
I gave Him all the praise to my wife, Marguerite
and the children.
Our constant closeness, especially our daily luncheons together as a family,
reinforced us all.
MADAME SPEAKER,
As far back as 1953, there has been the P.L. P.,
my extended family.
I will like to take the journey back and thank those, who have been loyal
way back.
Let's be faithful to all as we battle out our fears.
MADAME SPEAKER,
I'm proud to say my two fold mission was fulfilled,
known as "Bahamianization."
Looking back on all these successes . . . . Progressive Liberal Party.
To God give all the PRAISE!
Androsean you had never failed
to go "ALL THE WAY"
I know there's more to be done,
I express my deepest sorrow for failure and disappointments.
MADAME SPEAKER,
Therefore, as a member of this honorable house,
41 years of service as a member of parliament,
I'm done. I have reached the end of my political journey.
I have run my course, I did my best.

Twelve Visionaries

Prime Minister Perry Christie.
Mr. Philip Galanis.
Mr. Marvin Pinder.
Mr. Philip Bethel.
Mr. Hubert Ingraham.
Senator Obedian Wilchombe.
Sir Orville Turnquest.
Mr. Ervin Knowles.
Allengton S.P.B Allen.
Mrs. Cynthia (Mother) Pratt D.P.M.
The Hon. Frank H. Watson.
Mr. Bradley Roberts.

Thirteen Brave Patriots

Sir Cecil Wallace Whitfield.
Mr. Trevor kelly
Senator Janet Bostwick.
Mr. Preston Albury.
Mr. Garnet Lavarity.
Mr. Sinclair Outten.
Mr. Stafford Sands.
Mr. Roland Syonette.
Mr. Wilbert Moss.
Mr. Simeon Bowe.
Mr. Asa Pitchard.
Mr. Eugene Dupuch
Mr. Spurgeon Bethel.

Sir. Lynden Biblical Alphabet — Men

ABRAHAM was blessed with many descendants and the father of many nations. **SIR LYNDEN** was blessed as "Father of the Bahamian Islands."

BARTHOLOMEW was one of the twelve apostles appointed by Jesus to have authority over demons. **SIR LYNDEN** was elected by the House of Assembly 1956 to bring equal opportunity to the Bahamas.

CALEB was a man of confidence. He assured the Israelites the land of Canaan. Nu. 13:30. **SIR LYNDEN** was a man of his word. He inspired Bahamians to accomplish hope, and an unimaginable high standard of living in ones own land.

DANIEL was a man of vision. He interpreted King Nebuchadnezzar's dreams. (Daniel 7-12:5) **SIR LYNDEN** was as extraordinary visionary, who turned dreams into destiny.

ELIJAH predicted famine in Israel and raised a Sidonian widow's son. 1Kgs. 17: 1-7. In 1953, **SIR LYNDEN** joined the P.L.P. and helped to prevent poverty. He educated many to equal health.

FATHER . . . . Our heavenly father God loves us so much that he gave us life through His Son, JESUS. **SIR LYNDEN** was a political father. He loved Bahamians as he loved his family.

GIDEON was a 'mighty warrior' with the Lord on his side. (Judge 6:13.) **SIR LYNDEN** too was a 'mighty warrior' and we all knew God was on his side, we've come this far by faith.

HAGAR was a prophet who encouraged rebuilding of the temple (Ezr. 5:1.) **SIR LYNDEN** too was called 'a prophet' that left influenced on many. He architected the Bahamas.

ISAAC was a special son of Abraham and Sara. God promised him an ever-lasting covenant and a fruitful future. (Gen. 17: 19-20.)

SIR LYNDEN was an only son of Arnold and Viola Pindling. His promise for Bahamians was received, e.g. wealth, freedom, dignity, and power.

JEREMIAH was set apart from the womb. The Lord touched his mouth with words and appointed him over nations. (Jer. 1: 4-10.)
SIR LYNDEN was discipline and trained at an early age. The Lord gifted him with an outstanding voice that articulated words and many islands in the Carribean benefited from his knowledge.

KINGS . . . . are men who rule and take the stand in the land. (Ps. 2:2.)
SIR LYNDEN was a builder and shaper. He architected the entire Bahamian society. He fought for justice and equal rights for all.

LOVE . . . . JESUS is love. Bahamians know that **SIR LYNDEN** had loving spirit for all he met, and was thankful for his beloved public figure. He knew his people loved him.

MICHAEL was an Archangel and a chief prince. He helped Daniel with his vision for his people's future. (Daniel 10: 13-14)
SIR LYNDEN was the chief angel of P.L.P. He was the visionary who freed the Bahamas for the bondage of colonialism.

NICODEMUS was the man who came to Jesus at night. He argued fair treatment of Jesus. (John 7: 50-52). **SIR LYNDEN,** I believe, went to Jesus day and night with problems.

OBADIAH was the prophet who had a vision for many nations. (Obadiah 1). **SIR LYNDEN'S** vision made Bahamians dream and visualize for them self. His influence with the 'Caricom' made the Bahamas a part of the region

PETER was commissioned by Jesus to shepherd his flock. (Jn. 21: 15-23) He also delivers one of the most important speeches in the Bible. (Act. 2:14-41 at Pentecost) **SIR LYNDEN,** I believed, was led by the Lord in the early fifties to enrapture the Bahamas from slavery and its mentality. His most important speech was delivered on Independence Day 10ᵗʰ July, 1973.

RHOBOAM refused to discipline the Israelites with bad advice. They rebeled against him. He refused to give up on Judah. Years later the Israelites made Rehaboam King (1 kg. 12:1-24). **SIR LYNDEN** knew justice and wanted a change for all people. His inspiration and aspirations encourage ordinary citizens to accept the baton. The Androseans never let him down.

STEPHEN was the first Christian martyr of the church and full of the Holy Spirit. He was persecuted for his faith (Act. 7, 8). **SIR LYNDEN** was the first black Bahamian prime minister to represent the Bahamas in every phrase of society. He had unshakable faith. September 1983, The Brian Ross Report brought rumors against the P.L.P., but Sir. Lynden stood as an "honorable man."

TIMOTHY'S mother and grandmother instructed him in the scriptures. He traveled from city to city doing mission work (2Tim. 1:5).
SIR LYNDEN'S mother instructed and disciplined him in the Lord. He traveled the world with his knowledge and authority focusing on politics.

UZZIAH began his kingship at the age of sixteen. His fights were successful (2 kings 14:21-22).
SIR LYNDEN left Nassau the at age of 18 to study law at the University of London. He fought 'all the way' to earn an LL.B in 1952. He was called to the English Bar, Middle Temple, as a barrister-at—law in January, 1953, and to the Bahamas Bar in August of that same year.

VICTOR . . . . SIR LYNDEN was a Victor.

WORKMAN—one who does work. **SIR LYNDEN'S** work was never done. His single-mindedness was dedicated to his mission. He made great significant advancement in three main areas; health, education, and tourism.

ZACCHAEUS was a chief publican at Jericho. He was short of stature . . . . Jesus ate with him and he made the vow to give half of his goods to the poor. (Luke 19:1-10) **SIR LYNDEN** was the Bahamas chief counselor. He was short of stature with strength of a giant. He had consistency and persistency. He knew how to unite with the poor and the rich. He made sure Bahamians didn't go through much suffering as the Isrealites did after coming out of Egypt.

To Everything There is a Season, A Time for Every Purpose in the Bahamas

A time for change,
And a time to be honest,
A time for justice,
And a time for the law,
A time to love,
And a time for peace,
A time to be loyal
And a time to refrain from hate,
A time to be free,
And a time to enjoy freedom,
A time to be kind,
And a time to give,
A time to be honorable,
And a time to get rid of pride,
A time to committee,
And a time to keep your promise,
A time to work together,
And a time to unite,
A time for the new generation,
And a time to lead,
A time to go forward,
And a time to succeed,
A time to communicate,
And a time to speak,
A time to be wise,
And a time to have wisdom,
A time for God,
And it's time to go with Him,
'All the way.'

I Believe

I believe in the Bible
The importance of friends
The education that leads to success
I believe the importance of studying
The parents I have, living healthy,
Enjoying the simple things in life and loving everyone.

But legalizing abortions is ill conceived!

I believe in being responsible for my actions
I believe in being free
I believe in equality among humans,
Being different and unique
Integrity and sacrificing

And I believe in living everyday like it is my last.

Titles and Names of Sir Lynden Pindling

A Great Son
A Noble Father
A Loving Husband
Premier
Primer Minister
A Strong Advocate
A Molder
A National Hero
A Precious Gem
A True Champion
The Main Contender

An Irreplaceable Diamond
A Freedom Fighter
An Amazing Man
A Communicator
An Unselfish Visionary
A Legend
Mystical
A Loyal Politician
A True Friend
An Unforgettable Leader
Most Outstanding Bahamian
The Nation's Finest Patriot
A Moses
A Dynamic Visionary
A Man of Courage
Champion of His People
The Man of the Century

A Socialist
Man of the People
A Political Mentor
A Privy Councilor
A Visionary Leader
A Statesman
A True Bahamian
A Founder
An Extraordinary Man
Greatest Nobleman
A Special Man
An Aspirator
A Messiah
Greatest Bahamian that ever lived.

Melchizedek (Priest-King, Heb. 7) and Kingling

Melchizedek was not a descendent of Abraham.
Kingling descendent was not Bahamian born.

Melchizedek was a great man blessed by Abraham.
Kingling was a great man blessed by God.

Melchizedek was priest of God most high.
Kingling was 'high priest of the Bahamas.'

Melchizedek priestly calling was many e.g. to make right judgment for the people, guard the covenant and teach the people precepts and laws.
Kingling had many callings. He guarded the Bahamas lands and preserved minds. He made the right judgment on the 10th of January, 1967, with the 'majority rule' landmark. He was the man responsible for July 10th, 1973.

Melchizedek was knight of 'the order of Melchizedek.'
Kingling was bestowed that of knight commander of the order of St. Michael and St. George, by Her Majesty Queen Elizabeth 11 January 1st, 1983.

Melckizedek was a peaceful king. He wore a royal robe and headpiece.
Kingling had a peaceful royal reign. He dined and walked with British king and queen. He wore a royal robe and a lawyer wig.

Melckizedek was not just a priest he was peculiar, supreme and a sovereign royal ruler of all the universe. He was blessed a blessing to all. He was king forever. There was no other priest that portrayed a true priestly-kingship leadership than Melckizedek.
Kingling was not just a prime minister. He was unique and a blessing to all. There would be no other prime minister that would portray a true political leadership with such a legacy that will live forever.

Bahamlites Kingship

MOSES was the first distinguished leader of the 'children of Isreal'. He reigned for 40 years. Moses was the man God used to speak to the 'children of Isreal' and brought them out of Egypt. Isreal was blessed because of Moses's obedience.

KINGSHIP was a Moses for the Bahamas. God used him to speak to the House of the Assembly in 1953, and brought the Bahamas out of bondage.

SAUL was Isreal's first King. (1Sam. 15). He was a loyal worshiper to God and a great military leader. He felt out of relationship with the Amalekites, then his kingship began to decrease. He reigned for 40 years. He was succeeded by David.

KINGSHIP worshiped God at The Seventh Day Adventist Church. He had a noble leadership. His party the P.L.P. was defeated in 1992 by the Free National Movement and its leader Primer Minister Hubert Ingraham, after severing five terms (25yrs.) as Primer Minister.

DAVID was Isreal's second King and the first tribe of Judah. He was anointed by Samuel to be king after Saul's death. He was described as good-looking. He delivered the Isrealites from the Philistines by killing Goliath. He reigned for 40 years. Solomon succeeded him. (1Sam. 16)

KINGSHIP was the Bahamas first black premier defeated the United Bahamian Party in 1967. He was a good looking man with charm and charisma. God helped him with his most significant accomplishment, independence from Great Britain, and became the first primer minister of the Bahamas in 1973.

SOLOMON was Isreal's third king. He was the king who sent the nation to it's peak in power and glory. Under his rule, Jerusalem was embellished with several royal buildings and the temple of God. (1kings 9&15; 11:27) He lived in luxury and had hundreds of wives. He was the wisest man that ever lived. He reigned for 40 years.

KINGSHIP was the primer minister that put the Bahamas on the globe of glory. He orcrastra the Bahamas into a modern country Bahamas. He had wisdom and luxury. He was committed to his one and only beautiful wife, Mrs. Marguerite Pindling. He too had 40 great years in leadership.

I Believed The King

I believed the **KING** studied the leadership of many great philosophers, kings and presidents, and said like the apostle **PAUL**, 'I can do all things through Christ who strengthens me.'

"The good of human being was to strive for perfection and the highest good. Every person had to be well developed in both mind and body to possess virtues, courage, wisdom a sense of justice, and moderation or balance in all things." This is what **PLATO** taught. I believed the **KING** studied his beliefs.

One of the most influential and knowledgeable philosophers, who was the leading authority in western civilization on all subjects was **ARISTOTLE.** I believed the **KING** studied this man life.

"Know thyself and to get at the truth by examining one belief. Every question was tested and examined before advice was given." Beliefs of **SOCRATES'S** I believed the **KING** did not question Socrates' beliefs.

Who believed in justice during the middle ages? To whose death these words spoken, "To whom will the poor now carry their plea, since the good king is dead, who loved them so much?" **LOUIS 1X** (St. Louis). I believed the **KING** corrected these words.

Which king accumulated tremendous wealth and used come of his funds to paved streets and build hospitals in Paris? Yes, **PHILLIP 11**. I believed **KING** gave much to charity.

"I have a dream today. We shall overcome, we shall overcome, we shall overcome some day. Let freedom ring, let freedom ring." Yes, these are the words from the late **DR. MARTIN LUTHER KING, JR.** He was the Civil Rights Movement leader who fought freedom and justice for black people in the southern part of the United States. During the sixties both **KINGS** had belief that one day all God's children can shout, "free at last! Free at last! Thank God almighty, we are FREE AT LAST!!!

Prince Pindden

Prince Pindden knew at a tender young age that he had a great mission to fulfill. He was peculiar and extraordinary with goals and dreams, and went after them with 'black power.' He answered the call go ye 'all the way,' from GrandBahama to Inagua. His philosophy and wisdom was so developed and balance. Many were persuaded and got on board with him. When he traveled the island of New Providence, he'd inspired many to follow him. He challenged them to see his vision and help him accomplish them. The Androseans heard this exceptional courage speaker on Z.N.S., so they invited him to their 'party,' honor and claimed him with pride and joy. Later they heard that Prince Pindden and his followers were in the Berry Island spreading a message of hope. Their words vibrated along the Bimini Keys and an invitation went out to the disciples. Grandbahamians, knew they need a change, listened in to the 'good news' accepted. Prince Pindden knew he had God's blessings, so he had confidence and assurance to go 'all the way' across the Bahama land. Many tune into Z.N.S. to keep up with the mission of crew. When their flight landed in Abaco, the question was 'Do you want your gold mines flourished?' Yes! Spanish Wells caught 'the spirit.' The pineapple lovers in Eleauthera took Prince Pindden 'all the way' down to Cat Island. He went throughout the island with his energetic, loving and charismatic 'message.' The Obeah Man in the Exuma Islands had a 'black power,' caught the Princes' 'mystical spirit,' and the whole entire Exuma Keys were changed. Keys were tuned up 'all the way' with praise and admiration for Prince Pindden and his mission crew. Rum Cay and San Salvador were blessed by what they felt when the journey came to their islands. They prayed their blessings would go 'all the way.'

"Praise the Lord!" cried the Ragged Islanders, 'help us we don't want to go the wrong way.' New Providence was the landing strip for the crew, when ever the visionaries had to resume for mission. The multitude of people was always amazing. "We know our island is a long way from New Providence. So please, bring those disciples all the way to us," declared the Long Islanders. The land on Crooked Islands might not be straight, but the people there did something about that. They gathered the folks from Acklins Island and fellowshipped with Prince Pendden and his flocks. Prince Pindden promised every Bahama Island a mission trip. Distance was not a problem to fulfill a mission. Mayaguana was no exception to the followers. The island got nourished 'all the way' down to Little Inagua. The most southern island became strong as the journey became powerful and took Great Inagua 'ALL THE WAY' up north to its mission station.

That Night That Day

Oh! Tonight is the Prime Minister's night!
Where?
During the convention at the East St. Church of God of Prophecy
Horns blew, policemen, security,
Protocol!
Congregation stood proud
Oh what a night!
Excitement!
Lady Pinding pretty and classy
Mr. Pindling spoke as he stood tall
His voice, speech and charm
Oh! What a night!
Genuine loving relationships were established
When that day came to say good-bye
Where?
At the East St. Church of God of Prophecy
Horns blew, policemen, security,
Protocol!
Congregation stood proud
Oh what a day!
The family
The people
The speakers
The sadness
Where?
At the East St. Church of God of Prophecy
Oh! What a day!!

**BY: NORMA FERGUSON HILL@www.blackexperts.com
and daughter Jamie Hill**

Special thanks to Prof./Evangelist Ingrid Hart for her contribution to the book (Nassau, Bahamas/Cleveland, Tennessee). Also to Mr. Wendall Jones from Jones Communications International Nassau Bahamas for a contribution.

"Where there is no vision, the people perish." This book tells of a visionary and inspires others to become one. It is a combination of biblical, cultural, political, classical writing style, etc. all blended into creative poetry to tell some of the legacy and history of Sir Lynden Pindling and the Progressive Liberal Party. While reading this book, you will be able to see the comparisons of the Scripture and dimensions of Sir Pindling's love and passion for the Bahamas. "God has not given us a spirit of fear, but of power, love and a sound mind"—2 Timothy 1:7. This is what each subtitle demonstrates. After reading this book, you will have knowledge of what took place and is still occurring in the Progressive Liberal Party, and a creative way it relates it to others.

ABOUT THE AUTHORS

Norma Ferguson Hill is a native of Nassau, Bahamas. She is an anointed Christian and a multi-talented individual. She has ministered and worked in several islands in the Caribbean and the U.S.A. in various capacities. Norma is the founder of The Child and Scriptures Ministry. The author of two biblical books, she aspires a creative writing career and is very active in her community, and also the President of the Bahamians in Tennessee Association. Norma is a member of the Metropolitan Who's Who and has unique spiritual techniques and strategies to harvest souls for this millennium.

Norma holds a Bachelor's of Science degree in Christian Education from Lee University, a Master of Arts degree in Leadership Ministries from Pentecostal Theological Seminary both in Cleveland, Tennessee. She resides in Cleveland, TN with her husband, Eric. They have two adult children, Victor Hill in Nashville, TN and Jamie Hill in Chattanooga, TN.

Jamie Hill is an individual with intelligence, motivation, and dignity. She is a 2007 Tennessee Scholar graduate of Cleveland High School and has been recognized by the National Society of High School Scholars, National Honors Society, National Honor Roll, and Who's Who Among American Students. She attended the People to People Leadership Summit in 2006 at UCLA and was invited to attend the Congressional Student Leadership Conference Workshop in Tennessee. She is a 2012 graduate of Southern Adventist University in Collegedale, TN.

Jamie has also won a few awards for her poems from the Creative Communication's Young Poet's Contest, International Library of Poets, and the Society of Poets. She finds pleasure in listening to Gospel and inspirational music, writing poems, spending time with friends and family, reading novels, and traveling.